CCSS Genre Biography

MW00489871

Essential Question
What can people do to bring about a positive change?

Jane Addams
A Woman of Action
by Jane Buxton

PEACE

Chapter 1

Early Years

Have you ever wondered what to do with your life? Jane Addams thought about it for many years.

Jane was born in 1860. She grew up as the youngest child in a wealthy family in the small town of Cedarville, Illinois. Her mother died when Jane was only two and a half years old. Jane was brought up by her father, older sisters, and later, her stepmother. Jane's father, John Addams, owned several businesses and was a state senator from 1854 to 1870. He was also a **philanthropist**, a person who does charitable things for others.

Even as a young girl, Jane wanted to make a difference in the world.

Jane adored her father. She wanted to be just like him. Under his influence, she grew up to be **tolerant** and kindhearted, and she inherited his love of books and learning.

Her kindheartedness meant that Jane soon began to notice that people often had unequal lives. She could not understand why some people lived in big homes in one neighborhood, while other people lived in little houses in another. Jane decided that one day, she would live in a big house surrounded by smaller houses.

Jane's father, John Addams, was a successful landowner, miller, and banker.

Jane wanted to become a doctor. She thought this would be a positive way to help the poor, but Jane's father wanted her to get married and have a family. This was what most young women did at the time. Jane wasn't interested in marriage, but she didn't want to defy her father's wishes either.

Addams had a good education. She studied at Rockford Female Seminary from 1877 to 1881, where she developed useful reading, writing, and public-speaking skills. She was class president for four years and editor of the school magazine.

Addams (back row) made some good friends at Rockford Female Seminary.

Then, when Addams was 21 years old, her father died. Addams was devastated. She enrolled at the Women's Medical College in Philadelphia, but she could not concentrate on her studies because she was depressed by her father's death. Also, a childhood illness had left Addams with a curve in her spine, which made it painful for her to study for long hours. Then she became ill. Her illness meant that she had to give up college and her dream of becoming a doctor.

From 1883 to 1885, Addams traveled overseas. She went to London and saw terrible poverty there. She wished she could find a way to help, but what could she do?

In 1887, Addams returned to England and visited a settlement house called Toynbee Hall in a poor part of London. Toynbee Hall was an experiment by a group of well-educated young men whose goal was to improve the lives of poor people. It was called a settlement house because young men settled there to live. While they lived among the local people, they offered classes in singing, reading, and drawing.

Addams was excited because now, at last, she had a plan. She would establish a settlement house back home.

Extreme Poverty

Addams visited a market in London. It was the end of the week, and the market was closing. Cartloads of old, leftover meat, fruit, and vegetables were being sold cheaply. The food was already rotten, but thin, sickly pale people dressed in rags were desperately reaching for it. Jane never forgot what she saw. She wrote later of seeing "hands, empty, pathetic, nerveless and workworn ... clutching forward for food which was already unfit to eat."

Chapter 2

Addams Takes Action

Addams returned to Illinois, and with her friend Ellen Starr, began to search for a house to rent. They found an old, dilapidated mansion in the middle of a poor area of Chicago. Addams's childhood decision to live in a big house surrounded by smaller ones was finally taking shape. The two friends decided to model their Hull House on Toynbee Hall.

Wealthy, educated Americans were often shocked when they heard or read about the extreme **economic gap** between rich and poor people. Addams and Starr decided that Hull House would have two purposes. One was to provide a way for wealthy people to learn about poor people, as they worked to improve the lives of the poor.

Hull House was originally owned by a wealthy businessman, Charles Hull. The mansion had been built in 1856.

The other purpose was to offer the working people opportunities that were usually reserved only for the wealthy, such as education and music lessons.

Addams and Starr wanted well-educated men and women to come to live at Hull House. While they lived there, they would get to know the working people in the poor, rundown houses in the neighborhood. They would also organize lectures, clubs, and classes for the local people.

Addams had enough money to repair Hull House and fill it with furniture. She also sought money from other wealthy citizens to help keep the house running.

Life in the City

Industry was booming in Chicago at the time that Addams and Starr set up Hull House. Thousands of immigrants from Europe had flocked to America. They hoped for a better way of life and came to Chicago to look for work in factories. Many struggled to learn English and earn enough money to survive. Often men, women, and children worked long hours in poor conditions for little pay, while their bosses, the business owners, became very wealthy.

With great anticipation, Addams and Starr opened Hull House in 1889. Other well-educated people were eager to help, and they came to live at Hull House, too.

The house became a popular meeting place for local people. Hull House offered classes on many subjects, including the English language. After a while, it housed a theater, a library, an art gallery, a kitchen, a gymnasium, and a music school. It also provided many services such as child care, medical care, and legal aid.

Thousands of people visited Hull House. They were impressed by what they saw happening there.

Addams started clubs for children.

Valuing Traditions

Addams set up a labor museum at Hull House as a way to value older immigrants. They were able to use old spinning frames and weaving looms to demonstrate their knowledge of traditional arts and crafts. Addams said of the museum that "far beyond its direct educational value, we prize it because it so often puts the immigrants into the position of teachers … it affords them a pleasant change from the tutelage in which all Americans, including their own children, are so apt to hold them."

Addams became known as a kind, compassionate person. She was also an outspoken **advocate** for the poor. She gave talks to many different groups and organizations, spreading the word about helping the poor. Addams became famous throughout the United States, and as a result of her work, many other settlement houses were created in other cities.

However, Hull House needed money to keep going. Addams began writing books. She was a good writer, and her autobiography, *Twenty Years at Hull House*, became very famous. Addams's books made a lot of money, which she poured back into her work.

Addams wrote a total of 13 books.

Chapter 3

Changing the World

In Addams's lifetime, men, women, and children from the poor areas of Chicago all went to work. Most worked long hours for very little pay, and they were expected to work in terrible conditions. However, they would starve if they didn't work.

Addams heard of three children who were injured at the factory where they worked. One of them died. The machine they used was dangerous. Addams talked to the factory owner and asked him to put a protective cage over the dangerous machine. She was shocked when the owner refused.

Children often worked in textile mills like this one.

Children Are Cheap

Most factory bosses did not want the child labor laws to be changed. They argued that child labor taught children the value of hard work. They said that many widows depended on the money their working children brought to their households. The bosses also said that their businesses would not survive without cheap child labor. Child labor was finally banned in 1938.

Addams realized that she could not help all the poor people in America by herself. She could see that **poverty** would be an ongoing problem unless the laws were changed.

She began to talk with politicians in the state of Illinois, trying to persuade them to improve the laws about child labor, factory conditions, and the justice system for young people. Addams worked to limit women's work hours to eight hours a day and to make school free and **compulsory** for all children.

Changes didn't happen overnight, but people began to listen to Addams. Other citizens began to speak out against child labor, and attitudes began to change. Gradually, the laws were **reformed**.

Addams knew that it was necessary to change people's attitudes in order to bring about positive changes in society. While she is well known for working to improve the lives and rights of individuals, she also helped groups of people who were treated unfairly because of their race. She co-founded the American Civil Liberties Union (ACLU) and the National Association for the Advancement of Colored People (NAACP). Both of these organizations still exist today.

A Responsibility to Change Things For the Better

Addams believed that everyone has a responsibility to help others and to work to bring about positive changes in society. Throughout her life, she tried to bring about change in many areas of life. She worked for the rights of ethnic minorities and women, for improved public health services, for the needs of children and the poor, and for peace. She wrote: "What after all has maintained the human race on this old globe, despite all the calamities of nature and all the tragic failings of mankind, if not the faith in new possibilities and the courage to advocate them?"

Addams also tried to change the way people thought about war. She felt that war was wrong, and she tried to stop World War I. Addams traveled around giving speeches against the war. Many people supported her. She helped to found a number of organizations to promote peace, including the Women's Peace Party and the International Congress of Women. She became the first president of the Women's International League for Peace and Freedom.

The Women's Peace Party delegates sailed on this ship to the International Congress of Women in the Hague in 1915.

Some of the things Addams said made her unpopular with people. She received nasty letters, and some newspapers said disapproving things about her, but Addams was unstoppable. She kept doing what she thought was right. She couldn't stop World War I, but she knew that she was entitled to speak her mind, and she was determined to change people's attitudes about war.

Jane Addams is one of America's best-loved and most well-respected women leaders. She strove for positive change for people until her death in 1935.

Addams was courageous and determined. Throughout her life, she had frequent periods of illness, but she refused to let sickness stand between her and her goals. These goals were never for herself. They were always for others. In 1931, Addams received the Nobel Peace Prize in recognition of her life's work.

Addams was the first American woman to receive the Nobel Peace Prize.

Time Line: Jane Addams

1860	born, Cedarville, IL
1881	graduates from Rockford Female Seminary
1887	visits Toynbee Hall
1889	founds Hull House
1909	co-founds NAACP
1910	publishes *Twenty Years at Hull House*
1915	helps found the Women's Peace Party and organizes the International Congress of Women
1919	helps found the Women's International League for Peace and Freedom
1920	helps found the American Civil Liberties Union
1931	receives the Nobel Peace Prize
1935	dies, Chicago, IL

Respond to Reading

Summarize

Use important details from *Jane Addams: A Woman of Action* to summarize what you learned about Addams. Your graphic organizer may help.

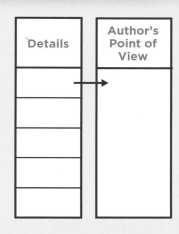

Details	Author's Point of View

Text Evidence

1. What type of text is *Jane Addams: A Woman of Action*? What features tell you this? **GENRE**

2. What does the author think about Jane Addams? Give details the author uses that reflect her point of view. **AUTHOR'S POINT OF VIEW**

3. The word *illness* on page 4 includes the suffix *-ness*. The suffix *-ness* means "the state of." Use the meaning of *-ness* and context clues to help you define *illness*. **PREFIXES AND SUFFIXES**

4. Write about the author's views on Jane Addams's work to have child labor banned. Look for details in the text that support your answer. **WRITE ABOUT READING**

Compare Texts
Read about a positive change for Mexican Americans.

Gus García
Takes on Texas

It was 1950 in Jackson County, Texas. A man named Pete Hernández had just been arrested. Hernández's mother asked the lawyer Gustavo C. García (known as Gus) to defend her son.

García was a Mexican American who wished to end racial discrimination in America. As part of this goal, he wanted to ensure that all people received a fair trial.

The law said that anyone could be on a jury, but in reality, Mexican Americans, African Americans, and women were never selected for juries. García felt that a jury that was so different from the **defendant** would find it difficult to be neutral.

Gus García was a civil rights lawyer in Texas.

García thought this case was a chance to help change the **judicial system**. He asked other lawyers to help him. At Hernández's trial, García raised an objection. He said that the trial was unfair because there weren't any Mexican Americans on the jury.

The judge said that it was just chance that there were no Hispanic people on this jury. García and his team of lawyers had done their research in anticipation that the judge would say this. They told the court that no one with a Hispanic last name had ever been on a jury in Jackson County.

However, the judge overruled the lawyers, and Hernández was sentenced to life in prison. García appealed, but a second court turned down his appeal.

García had one more chance to appeal. He could ask the United States Supreme Court to hear his complaint. A win for García and his team could mean a positive change in the lives of the Mexican Americans.

Poor Hispanic people raised money to help pay the costs of the case. García's team submitted their appeal to the Supreme Court, and in 1954, the lawyers appeared in front of the Justices. This court had never made a decision about the rights of Mexican Americans before. García spoke so powerfully that the Justices were riveted.

The Supreme Court building is located in Washington D.C.

The United States Supreme Court Justices announced that Hernández would be tried again. This time, he would be tried before a jury that included Mexican Americans and people from other previously excluded groups. García and his team had made history. This was also a victory for all citizens of the United States of America because it ensured that everyone could be part of the judicial process.

Endnote: At his second trial, Pete Hernández was found guilty again.

Make Connections

Why was García so concerned about changing the jury system in Texas? ESSENTIAL QUESTION

What personal qualities did Jane Addams and Gus García both have? TEXT TO TEXT

Ed Clark/Time & Life Pictures/Getty Images

Glossary

advocate *(AD-vuh-kuht)* someone who supports or promotes the interests of someone else *(page 9)*

compulsory *(kum-PUHL-suh-ree)* required to do *(page 11)*

defendant *(di-FEN-duhnt)* the person who is being accused in court *(page 16)*

economic gap *(e-kuh-NAHM-ik gap)* the difference between the incomes of the rich and the poor *(page 6)*

judicial system *(jew-DI-shuhl SIS-tuhm)* the courts and the branch of government that enforces laws *(page 17)*

philanthropist *(fuh-LAN-thruh-pist)* a person who cares about humankind and does kind and charitable deeds *(page 2)*

poverty *(PAH-vuhr-tee)* the state of being very poor *(page 11)*

reformed *(ri-FORMD)* changed for the better *(page 11)*

tolerant *(TAH-luh-ruhnt)* accepting differences *(page 3)*

Index

Focus on
Social Studies

Purpose To understand how changes in the past have made a difference to our lives today

What to Do

Step 1 With a small group, discuss what life would be like if you lived 100 years ago and had to work in a factory every day. Use the text and other sources for information.

Step 2 Make a two-column chart on a piece of paper. Label one column "100 Years Ago." Then write an imaginary daily schedule for your day 100 years ago. Don't forget that your day might begin even before sunrise.

Step 3 Label the second column "Today" and write your typical daily schedule. Include the things you learn at school, the things you do after school, and your evening routines.

Step 4 Discuss the two schedules with your group, noticing the things that are the same and the things that are different.